Hiding Places by Kathleen Trock

Photography by
Rachel Curet (pages 2, 40, and 41)
Tim Fleck (pages 4–11, 14–27, 30–31, 33–37, and 39)
Tim Pollard (pages 48 and 51)
Gretchen Stibolt (pages 12–13 and 32)
Kathleen Trock (page 47)

Book Design and Layout by
Gretchen and Michele Stibolt
Laura Sebold

Drawings on Cover and Pages 42–45 by
Eduardo Quintal Guillermo

All Other Children's Art by
The Students of Compass Fine Arts Academy, Elgin, Illinois

A Giant Thank You to
All of the children who share their hiding places with those they trust

Published by
This Joy! Books, P.O. Box 823, Elgin, Illinois 60121
A division of Three Cord Ministries, Inc., Libertyville, Illinois 60048
www.thisjoybooks.com
for Pebbles and Stones, P.O. Box 272, Jenison, MI 49428
1-877-705-9571, Info@PebblesandStones.com
www.PebblesandStones.com

Scripture taken from the Holy Bible, NEW INTERNATIONAL READER'S VERSION®. Copyright © 1996, 1998 International Bible Society. All rights reserved throughout the world. Used by permission of International Bible Society.

NEW INTERNATIONAL READER'S VERSION® and NIrV® are registered trademarks of International Bible Society. Use of either trademark for the offering of goods or services requires the prior written consent of International Bible Society.

Scripture on back cover taken from *The Message*. Copyright © 1993, 1994, 1995, 1996, 2000, 2001, 2002. Used by permission of NavPress Publishing Group.

Printed by Dickinson Press, Inc., Grand Rapids, Michigan, USA / August 2009, Print Code 3566700

International Standard Book Number: 978-0-9821835-4-0

1 2 3 4 5 6 7 8 9 10 / 15 14 13 12 11 10 09

Hiding Places

*Wilma Schneider
gave this to the kids
at our 2012 missions
Convention. (She ate
Supper with us)*

Kathleen Trock

This
JOY!
Books

Elgin, Illinois

Dedicated to God, our Father,
who puts in us the desire to find
our hiding place in Him
and to every child
who is looking for this hiding place.

Do you have a favorite
hiding place?

Jennifer does.
Just for fun,
she likes to hide
under the covers
and imagine
talking dogs,
singing flowers,
hollow logs filled with
delicious candy,
and faraway lands
with giant giraffes
and wide rivers.

6

Chris likes hiding, too.
In a game of hide-and-seek,
he slips into the tall cornstalks,
holds his breath,
and quietly listens to hear,

"1,2 3"

". . . ready or not, here I come!"

At Leticia's surprise birthday party,
her excited friends hide
behind the furniture
waiting to shout,
"Happy Birthday!
Surprise! Surprise!
Surprise!"

"Look at me! Look at me!"
shouts Moriah, lifting her hands.
Suddenly, her bike's front tire
wobbles, and Moriah falls onto the
pavement. Taking one look at
her scraped knee, she limps
into the open arms of
her father to hide
her tears.

Alex hides too.

Zigging and zagging
across the night sky,
lightning flashes a warning,
and the clouds answer
with crashing booms.
Trembling, Alex scrambles
under the bed to hide
from the storm.

Luke is afraid to take a test at school.
He searches for a hiding place by saying,
"Mom, I'm too sick to go to school today."

CRAYONS

Brittany gets bored reading to her sister
and begins kicking her soccer ball instead.
When the ball crashes into her mother's favorite vase,
a voice calls from the kitchen,
"What's going on in there?"

Brittany hides by answering,
"Erin did it."

Antoine walks on his tiptoes
and stretches out his shoulders,
hoping that the others
will quit calling him "Shorty"—
but the teasing doesn't stop.
He finds a place to hide
by being shy.

Anne and Mercedes
are sharing secrets
together in the park.
When Mercedes hears
Tonya calling her name,
she turns away from Anne saying,
"I don't want to talk to YOU
anymore."

Hiding her feelings,
Anne answers,
"Fine! Be that way!
See if I care."

Robert hears his parents arguing again.
He turns up the volume on his video game
to drown out their voices.

He hides in the sounds of the speeding race cars.

Whenever Maria has
scary memories
or fearful thoughts,
she stops talking.

When her friends ask, "Maria, what's
wrong?" she hides in silence.

And when Ethan hears
the sound of pounding feet
coming closer,
he presses his body
against a building
and hides
until the bullies
go away.

All of us have hiding places.

Jennifer liked hiding
under the covers.

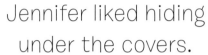

Leticia's friends
delighted in hiding
behind the
furniture,

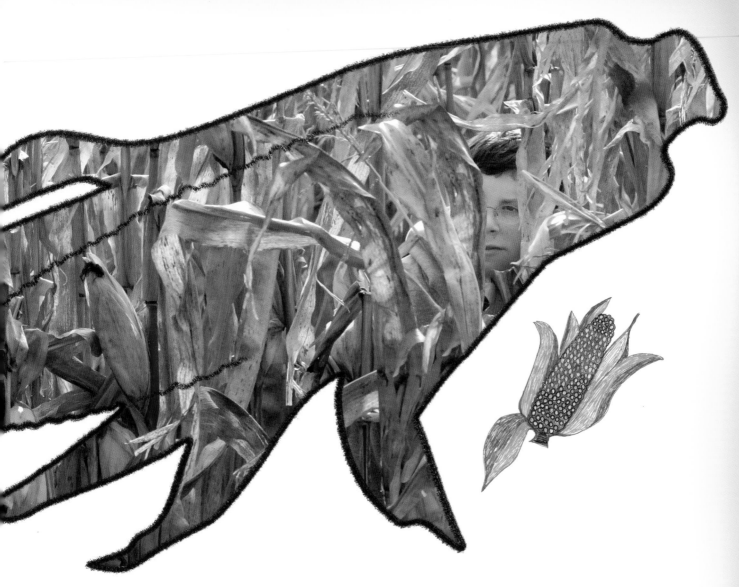

and Chris had fun hiding among the tall cornstalks.

Where do you hide for fun?

Alex felt safe under his bed,

and Ethan hoped the side of
the building would be a safe place.

Where do you hide
when you want to be safe?

Maria withdrew
from her friends,
and Brittany and Luke lied.

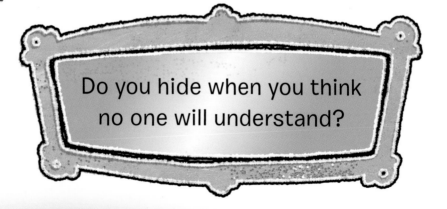

Do you hide when you think
no one will understand?

When Antoine stopped talking and Robert turned up the volume on his video game, they were still hurting inside.

Where do you hide
when you're hurting or sad?

All of us need a place to hide—but where?

Long ago,
a shepherd boy
named David
said to God,
"You are my hiding place,
You will keep me safe
from trouble . . ."

PSALM 32:7a

When David needed
a hiding place,
he talked with God,
and God showed David
where to hide
and what to do.
God gave him courage
to speak the truth.
He gave him peace
when he was afraid
and called David
His friend.

Like David,
you can talk with God
anytime or anywhere.
God is always listening.

41

One day a boy named Eduardo did just that.

He sat down to talk with God about his friends.
Sometimes they asked him to do things that were wrong.
As he told God how he felt,
he drew a picture of fish.

Every fish was swimming in the same direction—
except for one.

Eduardo asked God,
"Is that fish me?
Am I swimming
in the right direction?"

He sensed God saying,

"Yes, Eduardo, that fish is you.
I want you to follow me, even when your friends do not."

As he listened,
Eduardo began to feel safe,
as if he were in
a special hiding place.

When he shared his drawing with others,
they prayed for him and encouraged him to follow God.

Like David and Eduardo,
you can talk with God, too!

God hears you—
wherever you are.

When you want to hide,
talk with God about it.

When others make fun of you
or don't understand, tell God about it
and listen for the names He calls you,
names like . . .

Beloved

Precious

Wonderful.

God listens
when you share
your feelings
with Him;
nothing is too big
or too small for God.
He knows you need
a hiding place.
So the next time you
need a hiding place,
remember—

God is there!

Ask God to be your hiding place as you read these verses.

I am the LORD your God.
I take hold of your right hand.
I say to you, "Do not be afraid.
I will help you."
ISAIAH 41:13

I have chosen you.
I have not turned my back on you.
So do not be afraid. I am with you.
Do not be terrified. I am your God.
I will make you strong and help you.
My powerful right hand
will take good care of you.
ISAIAH 41:9b-10

God is our place of safety.
He gives us strength.
He is always there to help us
in times of trouble.
PSALM 46:1

God hear me as I tell you my problem.
Don't let my enemies kill me.
Hide me from those
who make evil plans against me.
Hide me from that crowd of people
who are doing evil.
PSALM 64:1-2

I know that
the LORD is always with me.
He is at my right hand.
I will always be secure.
PSALM 16:8

Trust in Him at all times, you people.
Tell Him all of your troubles.
God is our place of safety.
PSALM 62:8

You are my hiding place.
You will keep me safe from trouble.
PSALM 32:7a

When you lie down,
you won't be afraid.
When you lie down,
you will sleep soundly.
Don't be terrified by sudden trouble.
PROVERBS 3:24-25a

HOLY BIBLE

A Note for Friends of Children

In the beginning, God created Adam and Eve: they had no need to hide.
They were hidden in their Creator and lived in communion with Him.

After Adam and Eve's fall, their first act was to hide and cover themselves.
Despite their fallen nature, God still desired to be with Adam and Eve.
So, he asked them a question of eternal magnitude which continues to echo
throughout the fallen world, "Where are you?" (Genesis 3:9a)

Adam answered, "I was afraid. I was naked, so I hid." (Genesis 3:10)
And so it is today that many of God's children still seek to hide when sin uncovers them.

Hiding Places is a humble attempt to help children find their way out of hiding
and say with David, "You are my hiding place" and with Paul proclaim, "I am hidden in Christ."

Endorsements

"Not only children, but adults need a 'hiding place,' a place of safety. On a daily basis I work with victims of child abuse and neglect, spousal battering, bullying, and even of attempted murder. Oh, that they would all know, at a heart level, Kathleen's wonderful and delightful truth that every child can find a hiding place in our precious and loving Father. Each of us, in our own way, is a child, has an inner child, and needs that hiding place. Thank you, Kathleen, for this beautiful reminder."

Dr. Joseph Ozawa, Clinical Psychologist, Courts of Singapore

"Bravo! What a love-filled, delightful, child-friendly book. It will lead children to the safe place of God's warm embrace. It will teach young and old alike the value of listening to God and experiencing His loving presence. I highly recommend this resource."

Judith E. King, LMSW, ACSW, Clinical Social Worker

"This is a lovely book with a needed message—no matter what life events throw a child into fear, s/he is never alone in the process. God's promise is that we have a loving, gentle, Holy Presence who is always ready to listen and to guide us in our confusion. We have the ultimate Hiding Place in the One who loves us best. And in the Body of Christ here on earth, we have a circle of caring when we hurt. As children of God, we can all take comfort in that—no matter what our age!"

Joanne G. Halt, M.A., Spiritual Director at Stillpoint Center for Spiritual Development (Interfaith)

"Kathleen Trock has the God-ordained gift of ministering to the psychosocial challenges of children in a language they can understand and adults can benefit from. Her timely use of Scripture only adds to her empathic approach to capturing the mind of a child. In *Hiding Places* Kathleen demonstrates her depth of wisdom, her sensitivity to the human dilemma, and her belief that God is the source of all strength and healing. The adult reader will come away with a greater respect for the courage of children."

Sherrill McMillan, Ph.D., Ordained Minister, Licensed Professional Counselor

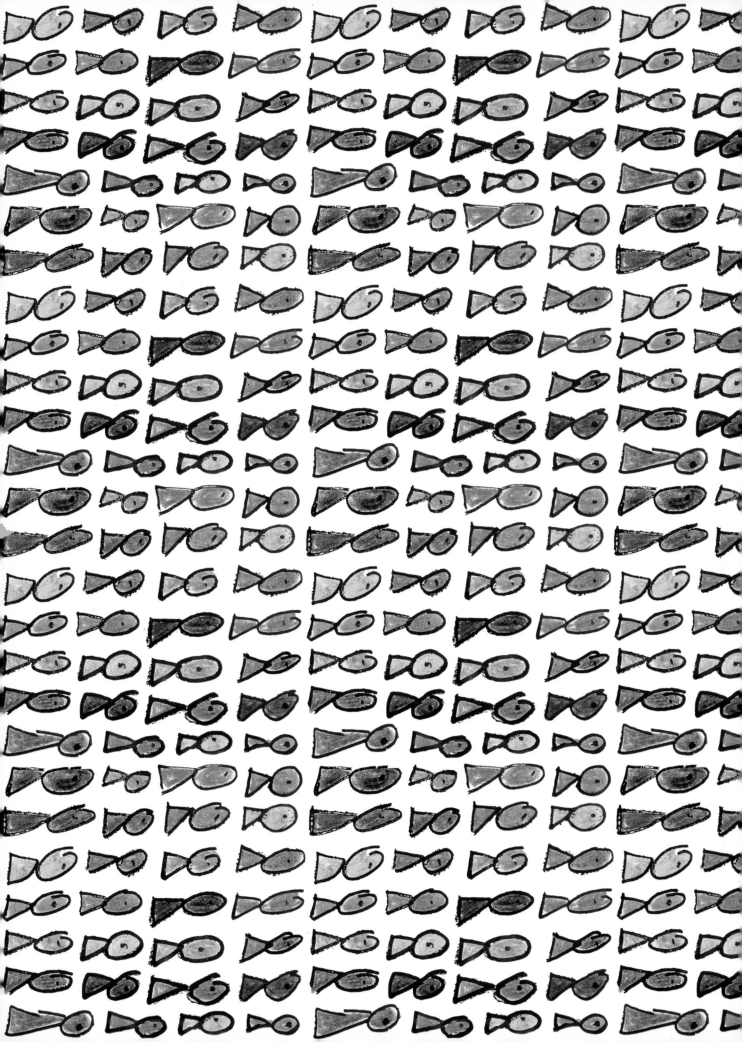